THE LABYRINTH

THE LABYRINTH

God, Darwin, and the Meaning of Life

Philip Appleman

The Quantuck Lane Press
New York

THE LABYRINTH
Philip Appleman

"The Labyrinth" first appeared in *Free Inquiry* magazine.

Library of Congress Cataloging-in-Publication Data
Appleman, Philip, 1926–
The labyrinth : God, Darwin, and the meaning of life / Philip Appleman. — First Edition.
pages cm
ISBN 978-1-59372-057-5
1. Philosophical anthropology. 2. Evolution (biology) 3. Religion and civilization. I. Title.
BD450.A67 2014
128—dc23 2013050428

Design by Laura Lindgren

Manufacturing through Asia-Pacific Offset
Printed in China

First Edition

The Quantuck Lane Press | New York
www.quantucklanepress.com

Distributed by
W. W. Norton & Company
500 Fifth Avenue, New York, NY 10110
www.wwnorton.com

W. W. Norton & Company Ltd.,
Castle House, 75/76 Wells Street, London, WIT 3QT

1 2 3 4 5 6 7 8 9 0

ALSO BY PHILIP APPLEMAN

POETRY

Perfidious Proverbs and Other Poems
(Prometheus Books, 2011)

Karma, Dharma, Pudding & Pie
(The Quantuck Lane Press, 2009)

New and Selected Poems: 1956–1996
(University of Arkansas Press, 1996)

Let There Be Light (HarperCollins, 1991)

Darwin's Bestiary (Echo Press, 1986)

Darwin's Ark (Indiana University Press,
1984; second ed., 2009)

Open Doorways (W. W. Norton & Co., 1976)

Summer Love and Surf (Vanderbilt
University Press, 1968)

Kites on a Windy Day (Byron Press,
England, 1967)

FICTION

Apes and Angels (G. P. Putnam's Sons, 1989)

Shame the Devil (Crown Publishers, 1981)

In the Twelfth Year of the War (G. P. Putnam's Sons, 1970)

NONFICTION

The Silent Explosion (Beacon Press, 1965)

EDITED WORKS

Darwin (W. W. Norton & Co., 1970; 2001)

The Origin of Species (W. W. Norton & Co., 1975; 2002)

Malthus on Population (W. W. Norton & Co., 1976; 2004)

1859: Entering an Age of Crisis (Indiana University Press, 1959)

Victorian Studies (founding co-editor, 1957–1963)

for Margie
now, and always

THE LABYRINTH

The simpler the society, the cruder the problems: we can imagine Neanderthals crouching in fear—of the tiger, of the dark, of thunder—but we do not suppose they had the leisure for exquisite neuroses.

We have changed all that. Replete with leisure time and creature comforts, but nervously dependent on a network of unfathomable technologies, impatient with our wayward social institutions, repeatedly betrayed by our "spiritual" leaders, and often deceived by our own extravagant hopes, we wander the labyrinth asking ourselves: what went wrong?

The answers must begin with our expectations. What is it we want? And why? What kind of people are we?

A beast condemned to be more than a beast: that is the human condition. Our anatomy, the fossil record, and our genetic blueprint all make our lineage increasingly clear. As Charles Darwin revealed to us, we are indeed half brothers to the gorilla, cousins to the other mammals, relatives of all the vertebrates. (And also distant kin to corn and to corn borers, to bacteria and to penicillin.) The structure of our bones testifies to our genealogy: the hand of a human is formed on the same pattern as the hand of an orangutan, the flipper of a seal, the wing of a bat. Embryology tells us more: the human embryo is virtually indistinguishable from that of a tortoise or a dog or a chicken. And our DNA defines and identifies us. We share over ninety-eight percent of our genetic heritage with our close relative the chimpanzee.

Slowly diverging from our forebears in the course of human evolution, we gradually developed a large brain capable of making generalizations and abstractions, of theorizing, of imagining things. Half animal, half aspiration, we were never as big as a bear, as speedy as a wolf, or as powerful as a lion; but we routed all of those competitors because the large brain proved to be the ultimate weapon: it made us the supreme tool-using and arms-bearing animal. The hairy mammoth, so huge as to seem invulnerable, became our prey.

Every gain carries loss on its back. The brain that could imagine a useful tool could also imagine spiritual kingdoms and invent a "divine" creation. In this primal fiction, the human species assigned itself the role of Chosen People. The other animals, our biological family, became in this perspective mere fodder, and we presumed to dominion over the fish of the sea, and over the fowl of the air, and over every living thing that moves upon the earth.

Our loss of innocence was not to have devoured an apple; it was to have made the chauvinistic assumption that all other living things are expendable and subject to our whims. Once lost, innocence cannot be recovered. It remains to be seen whether maturity or wisdom can replace it; as a species, we have hardly ever tested those qualities.

Divine right is a convenient argument for imperialists. *Deus vult*, "God wills it," serves not only aggressor nations but aggressor species too. The human assault on the plant and animal kingdoms has always been based on the explicit or implicit assumption of divine authority—an assumption so arrogant and so dissociated from reality that it is inherently unstable and self-destructive.

Clinging to our "divine" prerogatives, we cannot avoid that devastation. In our fantasies of godlike superiority are the seeds of neurosis, and when they bear their dragon fruit we run for the mind healers.

—•••—

The mind healers instruct us in what we already know: that we begin our lives in total helplessness but with boundless desire; that our dependency, and therefore this inner contradiction, persist for many years; that we cannot escape this dilemma unless we develop a sense of objective reality, a willingness to postpone desire, to limit our craving, and to channel our energies in useful, or anyway socially acceptable, activities. We have to acknowledge that there is a world of living things around us deserving our attention and respect.

If we cannot make that adjustment to external reality, we fall prey to anxiety, a straitjacket that restricts our ability to make reasonable choices. Then the unreal becomes our reality, and we grope our way through that labyrinth, pursued by the terrors of our own imagination.

The large brain is the ultimate weapon, and sometimes it is aimed at us. We are capable of abstractions, capable of imagining things; that is part of the problem.

We imagine all sorts of useful and pleasant things: wheels, shoes, poems. But the imagination refuses to stop before it is too late and proceeds to invent sinister hells, and sumptuous heavens, and miscellaneous hypotheses, such as "God."

"God" is an unnecessary hypothesis, but for many people, suffering the terrors of the imagination, a seductive one. People in general have never exhibited much passion for the disciplined pursuit of knowledge, but they are always tempted by easy answers. God is an easy answer.

Why are we here? Where shall we spend eternity? The brain has become capable of inventing questions to which there are no satisfactory answers. For such questions, God is a convenience: the unanswerable question is referred to the undefinable Being, and lo, we have the impression of an answer, though in fact we know no more than before. This seems to soothe some minds temporarily, as an empty bottle may soothe a crying baby; the nourishment from each is the same. "God" is a term that deliberately masks our ignorance.

Whenever God is invoked, language and sense part company. For that very reason, God has practical and political uses that partly account for its survival as a hypothesis. Among its other conveniences, God has always comforted aggressors by blessing the carnage of battle; armies carry their own chaplains. God is described as that which knows everything and is all-powerful. If so, then there is no escaping the conclusion that God is ultimately responsible for everything that happens—for the Holocaust, for the carpet bombing of primitive villages, for the defilement of children, for slavery. Priests were on hand to sanction all of those activities: God is a serviceable bureaucrat.

The worship of the undefinable is necessarily illogical: "Praise the mercy and goodness of God for saving my life," says the survivor of an earthquake in which God, with complete indifference, has just brushed away a thousand lives.

The large brain, that masterpiece of evolution, capable of wonder but unpracticed in reasoning, throws patterns across the stars: Aquarius, Taurus, Capricorn. To invent these images is poetry; to believe in them is faith. God's survival depends upon our peopling the heavens with angels and archangels, chimeras of our banal imaginations. No wonder the prophets thundered against the sin of knowledge, the sin of pride. God depends upon our ignorance as much as any magician.

Learning is hard work; imagining is easy. Given our notorious capacity for indolence, is it any wonder that school is so unpopular, faith so attractive? So we fumble through the labyrinth of our lives, making believe we have heard answers to our questions, even to our prayers. And yet, deep down, we know that something is out of joint, has always been out of joint. How long? we lament. How long, O Lord?

The only answer from the clouds is that the Lord thy God is a jealous God. God is also, judging from his own written record, vindictive, tyrannical, narcissistic, bloodthirsty, bigoted, and irresponsible. It is hard to imagine why anyone would want to be cast in that image. And yet so powerful are the urges of anxiety and neurosis that people quite seriously wish to emulate this moral aberration. Why should that be?

Recall that the essential characteristics of the infant's personality are selfishness and boundless desire. To grow out of infancy and childhood it is necessary to adjust to the reality of the outer world, which inevitably means limiting our desires in accordance with conditions in the world around us. Straightforward enough.

Throughout the world, though, are embedded the booby traps of theology. The most dangerous of these is the seductive promise of an eternity of infinite delight, just what we have been painstakingly weaned away from in our infantile years. Now, once again, the priests deliberately tempt us with these blandishments, exhort us to desire eternal bliss, and make us feel guilty if we do not.

Yet there is no guarantee that we'll ever get that grand prize, since the distributor of the awards is the same capricious tyrant who flatly refused to explain cosmic justice even to one of his favorites, Job, and who informs us that eternal delight is his to distribute as he sees fit, quite apart from our merits and according to a whimsical quality called grace. God either gives grace and rewards us for having it or withholds grace and punishes us for lacking it. Las Vegas casinos give better odds than that.

No wonder, then, that religion, in pandering to our infantile wishes, unfits us for dealing with reality. No wonder, under such pressures, so many people become confused and ill, believing they are something they are not. No wonder they are so often reduced to a state of primitive anguish, calling for help to the barren stars.

The fact is that religion is not simply a maladaptive factor in our lives; it was specifically designed by its various priesthoods to be maladaptive, charging us to abjure "this world." Attention to an afterlife necessarily reduces our interest in this life, but the problem goes deeper than that: the glittering image of Paradise breeds actual contempt for this world.

So in terms of our personal maturity, the dream of heaven is an outright affliction. Given a fair chance, this life can be well worth living, but in the context of infinite rewards of course our small struggles and occasional victories on this blue-green planet always seem like petty stuff. Under the crystalline dome of our medieval theological heaven, life becomes a hothouse that nourishes frustration and neurosis.

Some examples are in order. Consider the religious people we have known all our lives. Consider history. Consider the daily news.

In the U.S. Army during World War II and afterward in the Merchant Marine, I encountered a lot of curious notions. One of my army buddies once solemnly advised me that I could cure my "weak eyes" (i.e., myopia) by washing them in urine; and one of my Merchant Marine watchmates solemnly insisted that "Some people would be real sons of bitches if it wasn't for religion."

The seaman who pronounced that bit of piety was, to my firsthand knowledge, a drunk, a liar, a cheat, and an adulterer. Perhaps he thought of these qualities as his perverse credentials for setting moral standards, the seagoing equivalent of the opinionated bald barber or the arrogant, cigarette-smoking doctor. And as I enumerate the liars, cheats, and lechers I have known personally, I realize that most of them were conventional believers, whereas my agnostic and atheist friends are mostly honest, kindly, generous, and clean living.

We may account for this divergent behavior partly on the assumption that religious people can "afford" to be immoral: all they need to do to exonerate themselves for sin, immorality, and undetected crime is to ask forgiveness, on the principle of the goddess Venus, who revirginized herself after every orgy. If God exists, the old saying should go, then anything is permissible.

Nonreligious people have no such easy out. Their moral accountability is not to some whimsical spirit in the sky, famous for easy absolutions: three Hail Marys and ten seconds of contrition. They must account to themselves and live with their own conduct; they cannot shift their shortcomings onto God's shoulders. Therefore they have to be more careful about making mistakes, and this leads naturally to an acute sensitivity to the plight of their fellow human beings. The social instincts, said the agnostic Charles Darwin, lead naturally to the golden rule.

Another way to account for the morality of unbelievers is that they are less perverted by the antisocial tendencies of religious thinking, including the seductions of fanaticism. Some people professed astonishment at the religious mania of nine hundred devotees of the Reverend Jim Jones, falling facedown in Guyana in a mass suicide-murder. And yet that act was a testimony to the very essence of religion: a wholeheartedly sincere belief in a personal redeemer.

In Iran, after the shah was dethroned, his priestly successors sent thousands to their death by kangaroo court and firing squad, an act of religious fervor proudly affirmed as such by its perpetrators.

These are by no means isolated or unusual occurrences. To the fanatical mind, the act of pure religion has always been an act of pure violence: the hanging of "witches" by pious Protestants; the massacres of Huguenots, Albigensians, Incas, and Aztecs by pious Catholics; the starvation of Armenians by pious Muslims; the slaughter of Midianites, Amalekites, and Philistines by pious Hebrews; the slaughter of Jews by pious Christians throughout two thousand years of "Western civilization."

And of course that characteristic religious fanaticism continues and accelerates today, so that in recent years we have witnessed all of the following.

- Catholics killing Protestants (and vice versa) in Ireland;
- Christians killing Muslims (and vice versa) in Lebanon;
- Muslims killing Hindus (and vice versa) in India;

- Hindus killing Buddhists (and vice versa) in Sri Lanka;
- Jews killing Muslims (and vice versa) in Israel;
- Muslims killing Christians (and vice versa) in Egypt, Algeria, Azerbaijan, Indonesia, and Nigeria;
- Roman Catholics killing Orthodox Christians (and vice versa) in the former Yugoslavia — and both of them killing Muslims (and vice versa);
- Sunni Muslims killing Shiites (and vice versa) in Iraq, and Shiites killing Baha'is in Iran;
- religious fanatics killing tourists in Egypt, killing unveiled teenage girls in Algiers, killing subway commuters in Tokyo, killing thousands at the World Trade Center, killing Yeshiva students in Brooklyn, killing doctors and their patients in Florida and New York and Alabama and Massachusetts.

Religion stalks across the face of human history, knee-deep in the blood of innocents, clasping its red hands in hymns of praise to an approving God.

World history is full of accounts of fanatical ideologies careening toward human tragedy, but rarely has there been a more forceful demonstration of the disastrous effects of religious ideologies than at this moment. And yet, in the midst of a worldwide bloodbath in the name of religion, Americans are being relentlessly bullied into an uncritical deference to religion by their clerical and political shamans. High-powered censorship campaigns by well-financed religious groups constantly assault our writers, artists, teachers, and musicians, our schools, libraries, films, books, and magazines.

There is also a very personal side to what we must consider "the religion problem." When we begin to think of our recent roster of ministers of religion, those "holy men," we encounter a veritable Chaucerian gallery of rogues and felons. For we now have seen:

- the Reverend Jim Bakker imprisoned for fraud and conspiracy;
- the Reverend Jimmy Swaggart humiliated in sex scandals and in violation of federal tax laws;
- the Ayatollah Khomeini and his successors lusting for the blood of a writer;
- His Holiness the Pope obstructing birth control programs in hungry, vastly overpopulated nations;
- Rabbi Meir Kahane making a political career out of religious hatreds;
- the Reverend Sun Myung Moon imprisoned for tax evasion;
- 162 televangelists under investigation for financial irregularities;
- thousands of Roman Catholic priests charged with sexual abuse, child molesting, indecent assault, corruption of minors, and sexual battery.

As a certain prophet once said, "By their fruits ye shall know them." To believe that religion keeps people from being "sons of bitches" is about as sensible as believing that a good washing in urine will cure your weak eyes.

It is not by their deeds, however, that the world's religions wish to be judged — or usually are judged. The most outrageous "religious" behavior is always absorbed into the spongy justification of means-to-a-good-end, and it is never the victims of persecution and fanaticism who hold the attention of the faithful; it is the towering cathedral, and soaring rhetoric, and official parades of good intentions. This perversion of perspective is the triumph of the Ultimate Organization.

Priesthoods begin in vision and prophecy, sometimes benevolent, sometimes cruel, but always somehow "spiritual," the product of some personal insight. Eventually priesthoods follow the trend of all civilized life, getting themselves organized and losing their personal nature, whereupon the original vision fades or becomes distorted, and the organization itself becomes the object of self-preservation, aggrandizing itself in monumental buildings, pompous rituals, mazes of rules and regulations, and a relentless grinding toward autocracy.

None of the other priesthoods managed all this as successfully as the early Christian clergy, which expediently allied itself to the secular powers and modeled its own structure after the most successful empire of its time, complete with top-to-bottom control and a self-selecting, self-perpetuating bureaucracy. Thus the "Roman" Church created for itself a kind of secular immortality sustained by a tight network of binding regulations, rigid hierarchies, and local fiefdoms, which people are born into, or are coerced or seduced into—and then find that confining maze almost impossible to escape from.

But with that pervasive and aggressive organization came the attendant problems. Small organizations may make small mistakes; large ones are in constant danger of making catastrophic mistakes, nationwide and continent-wide errors, vast programs of wrongheadedness and social depredation, all enforced by their organizational efficiency. So we look back and see the murderous Christian Crusades, with their millions of innocent victims; we see the centuries of European Catholic/Protestant wars, leaving behind vast landscapes of death and devastation; we see compliance in and justification for genocide against the American Indians; we see mainstream religious support for the institution of human slavery; and we see the brutal religious repression of valuable human knowledge by burning scientists at the stake or threatening them with barbaric tortures.

In our own time the Roman Catholic Church has made the gravest error of all, setting its worldwide power and influence against the clear and urgent need for sensible population limitation. Largely because of that influence, human populations are now well beyond the carrying capacity of the earth and are rapidly expanding, especially in the poorest countries. As a direct result, we see increasingly devastating human misery: hunger, malnutrition, starvation, poverty, illness, illiteracy, joblessness, and homelessness — not to mention the consequent degradation of our environment and the destruction of countless other species who used to share this planet with us.

In the midst of all this social and moral wreckage, the priests try to maintain a facade of "doing good," repeating their protestations of love and charity — all the while their activities are wrecking human lives and human hopes on a vast scale. There is a word for this kind of activity, talking about love while blighting people's lives: it is hypocrisy.

Consider the fruits of hypocrisy. If we truly believed we were being audited daily for an account in heaven, and that faith and good works were the outward and visible signs of grace, then of course the uses of this world would seem weary, stale, flat, and unprofitable, and we would turn our full attention to acts of piety. There would be little interest then in such homely satisfactions as good work or good cooking or good tennis. The arts would be viewed as trivial amusements or as temptations of the devil, and music and poetry would wither away for lack of interest. Love would be chastened and sex abjured for fear of irreverent fervor. Weeds would grow up in the cracks of the human spirit.

Fortunately, such consequences rarely occur, because most of the people who give lip service to religion retain a healthy skepticism about it. This is the benevolent face of hypocrisy. Except perhaps for a few cloistered individuals, nobody these days sacrifices many things of this world for the alleged glories of the afterlife, although gurus and holy books exhort us all to do so—and indeed if we were counting on an eternal reward, it would make sense to do so. No earthly pleasure, not even a romantic dinner or a Shakespeare sonnet or a painting of Cézanne's, is worth the risk of losing heaven. Yet few people are abjuring the world; we are taking the cash and letting the credit go. So much the better.

The trouble is, some of us can't seem to stop worrying about an afterlife that we don't really believe in, and as a result the toadstools of neurosis spring up in the dank labyrinths of our psyches. On the one hand, when we momentarily break free from the snaky coils of childhood teachings, we find ourselves fretting about our apostasy. On the other hand, when we sheepishly return to orthodox reverence, our self-respect is automatically diminished, and we regret the opportunities for personal growth and adventure that we are then missing.

Most of us need to be much tougher-minded than we are, more resolute in rejecting the bribes of the afterlife. Once definitely done with our adolescent longing for the Absolute, we would find this world valuable after all, and poignantly valuable precisely because it is not eternal. Doomed to extinction, our loves, our work, our friendships, our tastes are all painfully precious. We look about us, on the streets and in the subways, and discover that we are beautiful because we are mortal, priceless because we are so rare in the universe and so fleeting. Whatever we are, whatever we make of ourselves: that is all we will ever have—and that, in its profound simplicity, is the meaning of life.

Evolving from an earthy past, from a family line that was hairy, tailed, and arboreal, how can we presume to ponder the meaning of life? Yet the large brain is a restless organ, and it will not stop asking questions, even presumptuous ones.

We are equipped with abstractions, with imagination. The trick is to use these sharp tools without getting hurt. When they help us to understand the world as it is, we must be grateful. When they create destructive fantasies, we must be on guard. According to the old holy books and the old philosophies, we were designed by benevolent gods. Darwin showed, on the contrary, that we are the product of war, famine, and death. Pre-Darwinian philosophies were constructed on false premises and are therefore basically flawed.

Ever since Darwin we have known that we came this way not by design but by random variation and the directive natural forces of selection and adaptation. To go on looking for design around us, outside us, is a destructive fantasy. It prohibits maturity.

And yet design is one of our fondest imaginings, and we will not abandon it. If it doesn't exist outside ourselves, we will create it inside, in our work and our loves, in our art and our avocations. This is not a trivial endeavor: we stake our happiness on it. We create the abstraction of love beyond sex, and can, with difficulties, be faithful to it. We entertain the notion of truth, and set out to test it. We imagine freedom, and try to achieve it. We are able to control these designs because we have constructed them and set their rules.

If we come to maturity by recognizing what is outside us, we come to wisdom by knowing what is inside. Balancing our desires and aspirations, orchestrating our responses to the world we encounter and our initiatives to the world we create, we teach ourselves all we will ever know about the meaning of life.

To presume to understand the meaning of life—what arrogance! Just look in a mirror: we are all dying animals, flyspecks on history. Our lives are a speeded-up film, jerkily passing from childhood to maturity to decrepitude to death—the career of a mayfly.

So a philosophy of life must account for death, and so should a psychology. To the other animals, death is an accident. The large brain makes it a tragedy, and tragedy calls for reasons: Why? Why me? And reasons indeed the large brain has, reasons the heart does not know.

Some of them are make-believe, the mumbo jumbo of theologians; some are other kinds of wishful thinking. But now we are after the truth, nothing but the truth, and this is how it begins. Once upon a time, in the cosmic neighborhood of our solar system, a vast cloud of dust and gases condensed into a mass so hot and so dense that it became a huge thermonuclear reactor—a star. In its gravitational field smaller condensations became planets, and on at least one of these, after it cooled, rain fell, and primitive oceans formed, providing conditions that could subsequently bring forth organic compounds, then molecules, then primitive cells. Some of these eventually began to photosynthesize, and conditions were then well on their way to a splendid proliferation that later, by the process of natural selection, became ferns, conifers, herbs, and flowers; and also reptiles, birds, insects, and mammals—including us.

As the orderly processes of nature go their ways, genetic discrepancies frequently occur in living things, blips on the screen of uniformity. They are almost always maladaptive and quickly suppressed. Out of many discrepancies, occasionally one is useful or opportunistic, and new characteristics thus enter the gene pool. A dozen or a hundred or a thousand more, and then another accretion: that is how we crept all the way from photosynthetic algae to oxygen-breathing primates.

Nowhere along the way was any all-powerful creator needed to step in and shape things. The process has always run itself, and goes on running itself. So here we stand, after billions of years of stability and billions of years of change: human beings, upright and cerebral, capable of anything, the most admirable and despicable animal on earth, making symphonies and sadism, medicine and malice. With *Homo sapiens*, a wild card is loose in the deck. We invent names for it: consciousness, intelligence, free will. Like a sub-atomic particle, it is impossible to observe in a pure, unaltered state, but we realize that it is there. We think, therefore we are.

Knowing what we know, suspecting what we suspect about the compelling determinations of our genes and the stern persuasions of our culture, how do we square all this logically with the odd notion of free will? By recognizing that there are no absolutes in nature. A totally persuasive environment is a fairy tale of the mind.

The large brain can imagine a hermetic prison of the environment, but in the real world there are too many cracks in the structure of our conditioning to permit it to be a prison for the imagination. We imagine ourselves free, and therefore, within unknown limits, we are free.

We will never know precisely what those limits are. You see, says the mind, you are trapped in your labyrinth. You see, says the imagination, you are free. Both are correct. The Absolute has turned its back.

With that understanding, we can come to terms with the irreducible fact of death.

———•••———

Charles Darwin, after many years of hard work and illness, controversy and honor, lay on his deathbed. A biographer tells us: "During the night of April 18th [1882], about a quarter to twelve, he had a severe attack and passed into a faint, from which he was brought back to consciousness with great difficulty. He seemed to recognize the approach of death, and said, 'I am not the least afraid to die.'" His last words.

Living among the relentless Victorian pieties, educated to be a clergyman, surrounded by threats of literal burning hellfire, why didn't Darwin fear death? Part of the answer is that by the time he was a mature man, he simply knew too much about the world to be frightened by superstitions. The once orthodox Cambridge undergraduate had, he said, "gradually come... to see that the Old Testament, from its manifestly false history of the world, with the Tower of Babel, the rainbow as a sign, etc., etc., and from its attributing to God the feelings of a revengeful tyrant, was no more to be trusted than the sacred books of the Hindoos or the beliefs of any barbarian."

Another reason Darwin didn't fear death and hellfire is that he could not take seriously religious threats that were openly sadistic. "I can indeed hardly see how anyone ought to wish Christianity to be true: for if so the plain language of the text seems to show that [those] who do not believe, and this would include my Father, Brother, and almost all my best friends, will be everlastingly punished.

"And this is a damnable doctrine."

Throughout his adult life, Darwin took a deep human satisfaction in his important work, in the comradeship of his friends, and in the love of his family. That was enough, and he was not merely content with it; ill though he often was, he was a happy man.

And he was not afraid to die.

Death, Darwin knew, is simply a natural part of a natural process. Death is always out there, waiting. Only its timing is in doubt. Eventually we will have played our small part in the great system of nature, and have passed on, leaving the system intact. We are, we have always been, a part of nature in the same way tigers or termites are.

Priests and preachers in most religions refuse to accept this sensible view of things. "Eternal life," they cry—thus thwarting all hope of a mature personal philosophy. By promising glory in a glittering but unreal eternity, they sour our satisfactions in a brief but genuine present. They portray a God who supposedly plans all things reasonably and wisely. After all, if we are reasonable, surely God must be supremely reasonable. Our bodies, we are told, are temples, so we treat them with respect and look forward to our threescore and ten years.

But God, it turns out, has something else in mind for us, and eventually we find out that God is not only whimsical but also a vandal. After years of our taking good care of our tidy little temple, God suddenly and without explanation breaks down the door, smashes the windows, rips the paintings, and slashes the furniture. All of our lives we have been prudent—about diet, about drinking and smoking, about doing everything in moderation—and all of a sudden, without any warning at all, God shrieks in our ear: cancer!

What if you are not religious when cancer slips up without warning, threatening death? You do not fear death any more than Darwin did, but you hate it. You hate the loss and the sorrow of leaving behind bereaved family and friends. So in your mind, and in the minds of those who love you, there is a sharp pain, a conscious rage at being mortal. Ants and alligators must also die, but they do not face that fact with rage or regret; those feelings are human.

Religion says: console yourself, there will be another chance, another life. Two things are wrong with this. First, there is not a shred of evidence for it and, second, it is a sop, consciously intended to blunt our rage and regret, thus dehumanizing us. Our anger at death is precious, testifying to the value of life; our sorrow for family and friends testifies to our devotion. Every noble quality we possess depends for its poignant value on our natural brevity. Our final pain is mortal, and our own; we will not have it cheapened by the seductions of an alleged immortality.

Face to face with death, we realize that the meaning of life is inside our lives, not outside them. We cannot impose on our experience a meaningfulness that we have not ourselves built into it. Our true philosophy of life is whatever we choose to do from moment to moment. If we regularly behave honestly and decently to those around us, then our philosophy is a healthy and adaptive one, accounting for our lives in terms of our whole social environment. The sum total of our actions at a given time constitutes our philosophy of life.

Darwin on his deathbed could look back on forty-three years of devotion to a loving wife, forty-five years of devotion to a grand idea. At the end, he had one characteristic regret: that he could not somehow have lived two lives, so that one could have been spent in full-time philanthropic work. The mind is tyrannically ambitious; the flesh cannot keep pace with it. Still, Darwin was content. He had made his commitments and he had kept them.

If the meaning of life is simply the fabric of our whole existence, then no wonder our brief careers seem to us so illogically precious, so worth clinging to. Self-preservation: even at the molecular level, is there a kind of self-interest in all that nonstop microscopic scurrying? Certainly at the level of the amoeba there is, and "up" through the scale of living things: it's always there, the fundamental imperative of life: survival. Preachers may sneer at this, but notice: they continue to pass the collection plate.

If we are to make any sense of what we call moral principles, we have to begin with the basic Darwinian fact of self-preservation. At all levels of animal life, this of course means looking out for number one. But at "higher" biological levels (not to mention the ants, wolves, and other social animals), self-preservation also means extending our perceptions of survival beyond the individual: to the family, to the clan, to the tribe. At a certain stage of our social development, it becomes possible—indeed essential—for people to see that a more effective conception of self-interest includes wider and wider circles of mutual interest: the nation, the continent, the world. At that stage, we come to understand that our personal well-being is substantially dependent on the well-being of people we have never seen, and never will.

Yet even at "primitive" levels of social understanding, human beings (no doubt including proto-humans, for millions and millions of years) have recognized that in order to live together in communities—as people must, in order to survive at all—we have to have some basic mutual understandings, tacit or explicit, some ground rules that we try to abide by. As Darwin observed, these always come down to a kind of "golden rule": treat others as you would like to be treated. This very basic idea was undoubtedly worked out, evolved, as a social necessity, a practical understanding, independent of mystical insights. Its virtually worldwide acknowledgment makes it certain that it is not the unique property of any one culture, much less of any one religion.

Darwin was often successful in his hunches, not because he was lucky but because he knew so much, worked so hard, and thought so long and so clearly. Thinking about our social ground rules, he surmised that after millions of years of living together in communities, our social behavior might be to some extent inherited. Darwin called that "social instinct," the inheritance from our long past not only of the self-preservation imperative, the so-called animalistic urges that often make people extraordinarily selfish and even ruthless, but also of our tendencies for "good" social behavior: showing respect for others, fair dealing, honesty—and, by a natural extension, kindness and charitableness. If Darwin was right about that hunch, then we all must "intuitively" recognize basic "right" from basic "wrong" in any given circumstance; that innate awareness is perhaps the foundation of what we call conscience. Even if it turns out that he was wrong, we would nevertheless be obliged to pass along, as part of our collective social experience, those same tendencies.

Once our species had evolved to social consciousness and communal morality, people naturally began to express their social approval with praise and to enforce their disapproval with contempt, anger, and ostracism. The gravest social offenses required sterner measures, so societies everywhere had to prohibit them by custom, taboo, and law, with penalties for violators. The social policing of community ethics thus would have begun as a secular necessity, not as a religious function. By the time the talented Cro-Magnon artists painted the caves at Lascaux, those moral sanctions had no doubt long since been part of our evolutionary inheritance—tens of thousands of years before the Bible, before the Vedas, before the Dhammapada, the Zend-Avesta, or the Koran.

As a famous atheist once said, "If there were no God, it would be necessary to invent one." And of course we did: that is when our big problems began. Evolution on this planet is billions of years older than religion, but when religion finally came along, thousands of years after evolution had developed our social instincts, religion then co-opted our socially evolved good impulses and encumbered them with myriad disparate, controversial, and contradictory gods, priesthoods, scriptures, myths, and dogmas.

Of course, we also retained our so-called animal instincts, right along with our highly evolved social instincts, and some people have always been motivated more by their primitive than by their evolved nature. When religions preempted the job of disciplining such antisocial people, they tried to deal with them both by the promise of heaven and by the threat of hell. But neither of these sanctions has ever worked very well, which is why (among other things) totally immersed Southern Baptists always performed the lynchings for the Ku Klux Klan; why nice Catholic boys have always run the Mafia; why a devout Jew murdered his peace-loving prime minister; and why, in a notorious American election, pious white churchgoing Christians voted two to one for a declared Nazi. After five thousand years of Judaic jeremiads and two thousand years of Christian polemics, we find ourselves in what some people choose to call a "Christian nation," where the prisons are crowded with obdurate felons, most of whom believe in God.

The problem is not that antisocial people don't know what's right and wrong or good and bad. As Darwin suggested, they may even have inherited that knowledge, and in any case it is all taught and reinforced by our laws, by families, and by schools. The problem is not that they don't know, but that they don't care. Consider this opinion:

> *The earth is degenerating in these latter days. Bribery and corruption abound. Children no longer obey their parents, and it is evident that the end of the world is rapidly approaching.*

That is from an Assyrian tablet about five thousand years old—but similar laments are common throughout recorded history, and under every political and religious regime. Clearly a perennial question must be, How can people be taught, or

encouraged, to *care* about right and wrong? If not simply by precept, then perhaps by example?

Our social and political leaders, given their professed religiosity, might be expected to be inspiring social role models, but they have often failed in that service, partly because the economic and political systems they represent and embody have customarily been patterned not on our evolved social instincts, our evolutionary golden rule, but on our more primitive survival instincts. Most of us understand that our survival cannot be a matter of simple eat or be eaten; our survival depends upon widening our circle of mutual support. But opportunistic politicians and feral businessmen have almost always set our social tone and social standards, so it is no surprise that our evolved social instincts are so often overwhelmed by primitive selfishness and a callous disregard for the less fortunate. As La Rochefoucauld observed, we all have enough strength to bear the misfortunes of others. Other role models are needed. Let us look again to science.

We are always moralists, Dr. Johnson said, but only occasionally mathematicians. It is usually assumed that science strictly speaking has no ethics, that the gap between what is and what ought to be is broad and unbridgeable. But our ethics, whatever their source, can hardly emerge from a vacuum of knowledge; in fact our knowledge often tempers our ethical inclinations. Scientific knowledge has at the bare minimum a selective ethical function, identifying false issues that we can reasonably ignore: imagined astrological influences on our moral decisions, for instance. Science offers us the opportunity of basing our ethical choices on factual data and true relationships, rather than on misconceptions or superstitions; that must be considered a valuable service.

Beyond that selective function, biological information has often been directly used (and misused) to support various types of ethical thinking. Unscrupulous people have sometimes appealed to spurious readings of scientific data in order to bulwark their arguments; that is what happened to Darwinism when Nazis perverted it in an attempt to legitimize their racist ideology. It is an understandable wariness of this kind of perversion that heats up the disputes about race, gender, and intelligence today.

More characteristically, though, the growth of scientific knowledge has tended to have socially progressive implications. Factual knowledge of the physical world has on the whole been a better basis for human understanding, human solidarity, and human sympathy than were folklore or superstition. The old myth-supported notions of tribal and racial supremacy have been superseded, among the educated, by the biological knowledge that we are one people, one species, in one world.

Finally, the scientific temper of mind is itself of service to moralists, sometimes supplementary to, and sometimes superior to, our social instincts. It is the "objective" scientists, these days, who are often in the vanguard of ethical thought, who are, for instance, enlarging our understanding of the capacities of the higher mammals and of our moral responsibilities with respect to them. The fascinating work of Jane Goodall and others with primate societies in Africa has not only broadened our knowledge of primate behavior; it has, in the process, illuminated the kinship of humans and the other animals. Human beings, proud of the role of *Homo faber*, the creative animal, the toolmaker, now have to share this role with the clever chimps, who, we have now learned, also have a distinct sense of self, a consciousness of individual personality. No wonder scientists are beginning to ask, quite seriously, as Carl Sagan did, questions like this: "If chimpanzees have consciousness, if they are capable of abstractions, do they not have what until now has been described as 'human rights'? How smart does a chimpanzee have to be before killing him constitutes murder?"

There may be no absolute values in ethics, but there are relative values in the various existing ethical systems, and one could make a persuasive case that those systems that are not only the most altruistic but also sensitive to the broadest constituencies are, by virtue of those qualities, superior to the others. Richard Dawkins writes, "If I say that I am more interested in preventing the slaughter of large whales than I am in improving housing conditions for people, I am likely to shock some of my friends." And he adds, "Whether the ethic of 'speciesism'...can be put on a logical footing any more sound that that of 'racism,' I do not know. What I do know is that it has no proper basis in evolutionary biology."

Our arrogant primal fiction cast the whole human race in the role of Chosen People and reduced all other living things to fodder, subject to our whims. With a growing recognition among biologists of the ugly and self-defeating aspects of that archaic speciesism, we may have reason to foresee a future consensus that a narrowly species-centered ethics is inadequate, not so much to our emotions (which have almost always failed us in this matter) as to our reason, now under instruction by new biological perceptions.

In the well-balanced human being (that will-o'-the-wisp of utopian thought) reason and emotion would be always in harmony, indeed in symbiotic function. In the meantime, it is reassuring to discover that biologists, engaged in "objective" research, so often become passionate about their work, and about the world it affects. Our cautious and rational perception of truth, it appears, sometimes causes, and sometimes is served by, moral fervor.

None of this would be so evident or so pertinent to our lives if biology were not a science so thoroughly unified by the principle of evolution as to afford philosophical perspectives of its own—and that unification, of course, we owe to Charles Darwin. Evolution by natural selection continues to serve biologists in their professional work and to inspire them to earnest pondering about our place in the universe; some of the wisest thinkers writing about the human condition today are biologists.

Could it be that a fuller, broader understanding of our biological condition might encourage people to care about right and wrong? "The moral faculties," Darwin wrote in *The Descent of Man*, "are generally and justly esteemed as of higher value than the intellectual powers. But we should bear in mind that the activity of the mind ... is one of the fundamental though secondary bases of conscience. This affords the strongest argument for educating and stimulating in all possible ways the intellectual faculties of every human being."

"Many things are at hand," wrote Pope Gregory the Great in 601 A.D., "wars, famines, plagues, earthquakes... [but] let not your mind be in any way disturbed; for these [are but] signs of the end of the world." In other words, wars, famines, and plagues are not social problems demanding solutions but only ineluctable divine retribution. So the other face of religious escapism is social irresponsibility. "God's will" becomes a thin mask for social cynicism.

Writing twelve hundred years later, Charles Darwin supplied an unintentional gloss on that pope's remark: "To those who fully admit the immortality of the human soul, the destruction of our world will not appear so dreadful."

The diversions of the Romans were bread and circuses; in our time they are sensational crime, sporting events, the sexual behavior of celebrities, and religious escapism. Nourished on such pap, many people find themselves lost in the labyrinth of neurosis and succumbing to easy answers and seductive promises: the priests need not soon fear for their jobs.

Those rare women and men who seriously ponder our own dark ages rarely have illusions about converting the masses to rigorous thought; the poor in spirit have always been with us, and will surely be with us for a long, long time. Short of any quick conversions, though, there is still a value in the ranks of thoughtful people speaking out, testifying, for only an utterly hopeless cynic would surrender the distant future along with the present. Every small light in the pervading darkness, from Giordano Bruno and Galileo to Thomas Paine and Charles Darwin to Margaret Sanger and Elizabeth Cady Stanton is valuable and necessary. Like characters in a perpetual Chekhov drama, we can imagine a more enlightened future age looking back on our time with distaste and incredulity but nevertheless acknowledging those voices in our wilderness who kept the Enlightenment alive until humanity in general became worthy of it.

The history of law in the West, after all, records our gradual transition away from the traditional religious resort to vengeance and toward a secular and humanistic confidence in reason and social equity; away from religion-sponsored vindictiveness (an eye for an eye) and toward the secular and humanistic reasonableness of noncruel and nonunusual punishment; away from centuries of religion-sanctioned human slavery and toward the secular and humanistic ideals of freedom of speech, thought, and belief; away from religion-sponsored "blue laws" that required barbarous punishment for trivial offenses and toward the secular and humanistic standard of due process in all things legal; away from the Islamic practice of chopping off the hands of thieves or the Christian practice of burning heretics alive and toward the secular and humanistic goal of separation of church and state, so that the one may not tyrannize over, exploit, or directly manipulate the other, as they always had, before the humanistic Enlightenment changed things in the West.

Contrary to the popular cliché, we can and do "legislate morality" in our secular state. It is, for example, both immoral and illegal in most circumstances to kill, to steal, to embezzle, to lie under oath, to rape, or to abuse children. Although various religions proscribe many other offenses as well, our society has not felt all of them sufficiently grave or sufficiently public to warrant legal penalties. The above examples of moral legislation, however, have broad social support, and their moral imperatives are therefore enforced by the police and the criminal courts.

For a law of any sort to be effective, what is minimally necessary is a general awareness of its correctness, its evenhandedness, and its necessity. Attempts to regulate our personal habits by law have had varying fortunes. The attempt to prohibit traffic in liquor failed in this country because there was not a sufficient conviction on the part of the public that drinking was significantly harmful to anyone but the drinker (except when the drinker is driving, which is universally illegal). On the other hand, recent attempts to regulate smokers have been more successful because of the accumulating evidence of harm to others.

As long as laws are reasonable and democratically arrived at, most people will tend to obey them even when they know they can get away with breaking them: not killing, not stealing, not even running stoplights are all normally taken for granted. No matter how reasonable a law seems to some people, however, it will not be honored by all unless the society that sponsors it offers fairness and opportunity. "The law in its majestic equality," wrote Anatole France, "forbids the rich as well as the poor to sleep under bridges, to beg in the streets, and to steal bread." Millionaires do not commonly rob candy stores or push drugs on street corners; their offenses are of a more rarefied order. But as long as there is a permanent underclass, a substantial body of people who cannot find a way of sharing in the fruits of society, that underclass will always be a threat to the social fabric, because, although human beings can, in difficult times, tolerate hardship, they will not accept flagrant unfairness indefinitely; an aggrieved underclass will always be trying to "get even." Given that condition, there is obviously no hope of the religious mechanisms ("Be good and society will improve") working well in the long run; they will serve only to breed more neurosis. What is required is a secular solution, which works the other way around: "Improve the society and most people will behave better."

It is never possible to write all of the next century's laws; our consciousness of social necessity is constantly changing, and in the course of social evolution we can always expect some degree of controversy and turmoil. In 1860 a major problem in this country was human slavery, a burning issue then, vehemently defended by conservatives, slave owners, and most religions. Today, no one would defend the slave owners, and yet our current crop of conservatives is reluctant to allow advances in equity for those who have long been denied it: blacks, other minorities, and women. A generation or a century from now, people will surely think it strange and shameful that anyone should have balked at this natural evolution of rising expectations.

Advances in social equity, however slow and hard won they may be, help to sustain what we think of as "progress" in what we think of as "virtue." Humane and liberal societies gradually come to a more sensitized understanding of the plight of the less fortunate and devise sensible ways of assisting them; the underclass then feels less trapped, becomes less confrontational, and is less motivated to break the social contract. Good law and good customs precede good behavior. Practicing the golden rule turns out to be not only altruistic but also self-serving.

An equitable and humanistic society would stimulate something much better than mere conformity to social rules. In such a society, people could be encouraged to ponder their own lives and their place in the world; to acquire full and accurate knowledge of that world, unwarped by myths and superstitions; to assess human problems and act with reasonableness and compassion. Free from the racking fear of deprivation and from the labyrinth of brutal religious animosities, free from holy nonsense and pious bigotry, living in a climate of openness, tolerance, and free inquiry, people would be able to create meaning and value in their lives: in the joy of learning, the joy of helping others, the joy of good health and physical activity and sensual pleasure, the joy of honest labor; in the richness of art and music and literature and the adventures of the free mind; and in the joys of nature and wildlife and landscape—in short, in the ephemeral but genuine joy of the human experience.

That joy does not depend upon mysticism or dogma or priestly admonition. It is the joy of human life, here and now, unblemished by the dark shadow of whimsical forces in the sky. Charles Darwin's example, both in his work and in his life, helps us to understand that that is the only "heaven" we will ever know. And it is the only one we need.

ABOUT THE AUTHOR

Philip Appleman is Distinguished Professor Emeritus at Indiana University and has taught at Columbia University and SUNY Purchase. He has also been Visiting Scholar at New York University and the University of Southern California. In two yearlong trips with the International School of America, he taught literature and philosophy in twenty countries around the world. He has given lectures and readings in more than forty colleges and universities, as well as at the Library of Congress, the Guggenheim Museum, the American Museum of Natural History, the Folger Shakespeare Library, the Huntington Library, the International Poetry Forum, the International Congress of the History of Science, and many other venues.

Among other responsibilities, Appleman has been consultant to the NEH Project on Ethics and Values in Health Care, Columbia University College of Physicians and Surgeons; consultant to the Hastings Center Project on Applied Humanities and Public Policy, and consultant to the Indiana and Kentucky State Arts Commissions. He was a founding editor of *Victorian Studies* and is on the Editorial Board of the *Encylopedia of Anthropology*.

Among his honors have been many awards for his poetry, the Humanist Arts Award from the American Humanist Association, and the Friend of Darwin Award from the National Council for Science Education.

He served in the Army Air Corps during World War II and afterward in the Merchant Marine. He is married to playwright Marjorie Appleman; they live in New York City, East Hampton, NY, and Pompano Beach, FL.